# Lies

*21st-Century Edition*

by

Paul Montgomery

Collection and poems © Paul Montgomery 2012
with exceptions of I was at a, Dawn, Maybe,
Clarity+Distinction=Truth, Pebble Creek, Could Desire,
Journey, Love, Andre, Electric Lipstick, Song of the
Googolplex, Ice, Drupes and Bribets, The Gnarled Old Man,
June Rain, Hemlock, The Muse Pirates, Queue, The Viking
© Paul Montgomery 1987

All rights reserved. No part of this publication may be reproduced, stored in a retrieval system, or transmitted, in any form or by any means, electronic, mechanical, photocopying, recording, or otherwise, without the prior permission of Paul Montgomery or his heirs.

This book is sold subject to the condition that it shall not, by way of trade or otherwise, be lent, re-sold, hired out or otherwise circulated without the publisher's prior consent in any form of binding or cover other than that in which it is published and without a similar condition including this condition being imposed on the subsequent purchaser.

Cover art, Frontispiece, "Sheila"
© Paul Montgomery 2012

Jacket Photo - Ellen Giamportone
ISBN 978-0-988-20770-7
21st-Century Edition

Googolplex Publishing

*For Lily*

# Table of Contents

Love Affair
11

I Am The Greatest Poet Ever
12

The Secret of Life
13

There Is Not a New Poetry Plant Opening Near You
14

For a Call Center Representative
17

Cover Letter to Adam & Eve
19

The Neighborhood of Desire
23

To Men, To Make Much of Older Women
33

Gated Community
35

101
36

Autobiographical Poem
37

Breath Angel
38

Race Between Glow and Shadow
39

Richard Brautigan
40

Ode to the Moon
41

Music Box Catalog
42

The Religion of Life
43

On the Structural Mechanics of Amor
44

Breakfast
45

The Secret of Life
46

I was at a
47

Dawn
48

Maybe
49

Clarity+Distinction=
Truth
50

Pebble Creek
52

Could Desire
53

Joutney
54

Love
55

Andre
56

Electric Lipstick
57

Song of the Googolplex
59

Ice
60

Drupes and Bribets
61

The Gnarled Old Man
62

Hemlock
63

June Rain
64

The Muse Pirates
65

Queue
68

The Viking
69

Balanitis
71

Blizzard of '03 - Durham
72

Prayers Answered
73

They
74

Missoula Song
75

To the girl of a different religion who wouldn't date me
77

3 Variations on the 1st Line of the Tao Te Ching
78

One More Variation on the 1st Line of the
Tao Te Ching
79

Tragedy
80

Figoa's Law of Irrationality
81

TRAGIC CITY ESSAYS - Number 1
Muse Pirates in the Tragic City
82

Sheila
83

Hello
85

The Dancer
86

My love
89

Illings
90

Poemoep
93

The Branch Crack'd
96

Winter Snuggle
98

The Eternal
99

Torture
100

Agnosticism
102

Wind
103

Shhh! Poet at Work
104

Men
105

Life
106

Fragments and Aphorisms
107

# Illustrations

Frontispiece
1

"Sheila"
109

# Love Affair

I liked her
 more than she liked me.
 so it couldn't be.

# I Am The Greatest Poet Ever

I am the greatest poet ever.
        And, I can prove it for forever.
Because I can rhyme orange
With Julian Assange.
Now, ain't that pretty fuckin' clever.

# The Secret of Life

If you lost your father,
  to be a father.
If you were teased,
  to treat someone with kindness.
If you were beaten,
  to bind someone's wounds.
If you were hated,
  to love someone.
If you were ridiculed,
  to praise someone.
If you were despised,
  to teach someone pride.
If you were called names,
  to show someone their possibilities.
If you were neglected,
  to give someone your attention.

# There Is Not a New Poetry Plant Opening Near You

Poetry does not conform
to factory requirements.
Poetry cannot be standardized
and its results may vary.

Poetry does not provide
a living wage.
Poetry is not creating
new jobs for our economy.

Your experience with poetry
will not secure you a position.
Poetry is not hiring.

There is no new marketing
campaign targeting consumers
to convince them of
their need for poetry.
Poetry is neither new
nor improved.

There have been no recent

markdowns.
There are no significant
Savings.

Poetry is inimical to division
of labor.
There has been no successful
assembly line of poetry.

Once I visited a bookstore
at the mall. Inside, there
was a poetry computer.
It asked in whose honor
it should compose a poem.
I had it create a poem
praising Hitler's perfect virtues.

Poetry is not a significant
portion of the Gross
Domestic Product.
Poetry's value is immeasurable.

There are no tax breaks
 for poetry.
Why bother?

Poetry consumes scant
resources.
Poetry is hard on trees.

Poetry cannot be considered
 work.
Poetry provides no time off.

Poetry carries no health plan.

Poetry helps your heart.

Poetry demands your full
  attention.
Poetry pays you back in
  sand.

There are no stockbrokers
dealing in shares of poetry.
No banker will accept
poetry for your account.

There is no retirement plan
   from poetry.
     Poetry pays no dividends.

Poetry does not donate
proceeds to charity.
 Poetry is charity,
    and faith and hope.

Poetry provides amusement.
But, poetry cannot be considered fun.

Yet, if you listen
     to the voice of the muse
     as she's singing,
   You can hear a sob, a cry,
   a wail,
     A laugh, a chuckle, a guffaw,
     What a fool she's made of you!

# For a Call Center Representative

Can I be official
  without being officious?
Can I be glad
  without being glib?
Let me be serious
  without being sedate.
Let me be fast
  without being frenzied.
Let me be calm
  without being callous.
Please let me say
   what needs to be said
  without saying more
     or being a bore.
Let me be myself
  without being robotic
And show my personality
without seeming neurotic.
Finally, Please let me care
  And respect everyone's
     fundamental humanity;
    No matter who they are,

Or, who they know,
Or, what they say,
Or, how they sound,
Even if I want to reach
　　through the phone cord
　Grab their tongue,
　And, strangle them.
Even if.

# Cover Letter to Adam & Eve

# Do Not Open!

This envelope unless you are willing to hire the most creative man in the triangle.

If you are willing to settle for second best,
   If you do not have a problem with
                                    mediocrity,
If you are satisfied with your current level of
                                          sales,
If you do not reward or acknowledge your top
                                      performers,
If you like to spend all your time with your
                               worst & middling,
If you like to pretend all employees contribute
                                          equally,
If you ignore innovation or pretend the
                  exceptional is the commonplace,
If you don't believe that success is a choice,
If you want to treat employees like cogs in a
                                         machine,
If you like to create chaos and act like it's a
                                        normality,

OR, continually fail to recognize the
                            recurring crisis
And, Run like a headless chicken when a
                            little
   judicious planning would have you cuke
                      cool.
If you like to pretend I'm a cow so you can milk
                            me,
If you like to trick people when the truth is
                       more effective,
If you like to pay peanuts and ask your monkeys
                         to shave,
If you want agreement when discussion is called

   for,
If you reject investments because you've learned
                          to say "No",
If you don't mind if your story is silly and
                             foolish,
If you ignore your marketing department and
               wonder why you aren't successful,
If you demand loyalty and return it with the
                             boot,
If you are shaking your head at this letter,
If you think I'm a jerk and a hopeless poet,
If you claim to love creativity but hate creative
                             people,
If you expect the creative to not glimpse
                        opportunity,
If you make efficiency such an icon that you
                 create watery beer,
If you sob in your hands because the windmill
                         hasn't fallen,
If your injudicious use of confrontation has left
                     you friendless,

If you're not willing to take a chance on a hard worker,
If you think employee seniority is more important than productivity,
If you expect me to beg for office supplies,
If you wish to remain silent,
If you expect me to stop complaining when you want to hire an employee at more money when by buying software we eliminate the need for the employee;
That I will do but I won't be long for your business,
If you wish me to remain silent,
If my prowess with words, education and experience intimidate you,
If you think I want to jump ship when really I want a competent captain,
If you think I'm trouble,
If you ignore me and then wonder why I'm unhappy,
If you give me crap directions and then yell at me when I'm wrong,
If you want to touch every part of my project,
If you never want to hear customer feedback,
If you think I'm a pill,
If you don't believe that every company I have worked for has benefited greatly from having me as an employee and has always done worse when I left,
If you think ideas are a dime a dozen,
    And, employees are easily replaced,

If you don't care about turnover,
        Because, wages are low,
If you think you'll just ignore me because I
                              won't realize
    the value of my contribution,
        And, feel that if you did acknowledge me
        I would ask for too much money,
        So, you keep your mouth shut,
            and hope for the best,
If you don't think you're in competition
        with every other company out there
           for my time and energy and passion,


**THEN DEFINITELY DO NOT OPEN
THIS ENVELOPE!**

# The Neighborhood of Desire

I

There she waved,
That prune of a face,
flapping her dis-jointed hand
into the wind.
"Hi, I'm Mrs. Hart,
Virginia." she said.
We had soon twisted
her name to fit our minds.
   "Vagina Fart,"
She was dubbed.
"A face like Yoda,
    peering through the window."
   said Kork the unstoppable.
She was tryin' to be a neighbor
of her triangular block across the street.

Words flowed from the wrinkly mouth.
"She'll tell you her whole life story."
Came from my invisible cynical companion,

   Scott Phelps.
And on it came as if she had dammed
  this dirge of information
Waiting for my parched mind
   to soak up her march to the ground.
  "Marcus Daly," came out.
"Well, I'm doing a report on him."
   Information,
    Formation,
"Can I ask you some questions?"
More babble on life history
  and a table of Marcus Daly's.
Her father was his gardener
   up the Bitterroot.


     II


   Dickie
struggling to balance the third pair of sunglasses
 on his Nose,
  skin a milky gloss
  covering red and blue veins.
 The type of skin popular
  for women in the 19th century.
"I've had a cornea transplant.
  You'll have to excuse me."
"There's that Daly Mansion
  in Hamilton."
  "That's open to the public."
 "They might know."

"He said I might just
   confuse you but I'll just
    give you the general facts."

    Vagina spoke out.

"Hugo was down asking
   for a glass of milk,
    Course, he doesn't drink
      it usually."
And the twins
   however old they were
   and still living with
     their mom.
A southern belle
raised in the tradition
    At 82 a foster grandparent
taking the boys
   Kork and Mike
    the new roommate
   Out to Dinner.
   "Are we the foster grandchildren?"
     Page Two News
 Spoke of the Foster-grand parent's
     Event
"Only iniquity shall save the wanderers."
    Hugo said bursting out
    of the door in a rage
   A thin skeleton picked dry
    by the termites
  Vagina told lived in the house.


      III    C

The woman from work
     dropped by.
"Would you put our power in your name?"
   "Sure, Sure," said I.

Winter has wounded
        our bucks.
"One-hundred-and-forty for the new
        house." "That, It sucks."

Your name to which we'll
        trust dough.
"Why shake the fingers of your hands, so?"
   "Why?" said I, "No, No."

At the company
    I found,
"You'll have to put your deposit down."
      My teeth were ground.

The woman from work
     was bummed.
"My credit is shot, too. Sorry." My
    fingers were drummed.

## IV

    Shall I speak of my work?
I don't care for your answer
  so I shall, anyway.
I didn't really care
   how you responded
    for I'd intended
   to tell you this critical
   intelligence, which this poem
  so heartily needs.

   Yes, where is this work,

             that I have told
           you of my co-worker?
It is out-of-town
             not far away.
         Just out of sight,
          Up the Hell-gate.
        It's an old souls' facility.
             Packed in their can,
               I pried the lid
                 and peered in held back by the smell.
    "Packed in Urine." the label read.
              My nose, stung and stuffed,
                  crept up in my face.
                 Sleeping on a couch in the can,
My brain on hold for an evening.
The night creeps creeping,
grabbing a couch and sleeping,
        enangered to slap
            or nod a quizzical head.
"I want to go home!"
 yelled and screamed
         and pelled.
"I want to go home!"
     pled and bled
     over morning bread.
      "I want to go home!"
    "We'll shut you in the camper!"
Solitary confinement.
   Away from the sardines.
          Packed in her own flavour.
"I want some poison."
   "None Today." Give me
       that bottle. "How much?"

## V

Shall we turn to those Muse Pirates
        Again?
Blinding and Gouging Eyes,
   Killing Brains,
Splattering Words on the page -
White sheets in the wind,
blown lightly from the fire
    in the hold,
  These Crimson Blades
     Rend thought
       from letter,
      lunging heartily
     grasping the lungs
      and tearing the sacs
       from sacs, blood
          splashing on the deck.
    Cutlass in vocal cords,
        Windpipe slit from lungs
      to Glottis,
    tongue stomped and chewed,
    teeth broken from metal
      unbended, shattering in harder-
     than-bone shards.
Kicking the athletes and their
    cold codes
onto the planks
    on their faces.
Bending the musicians'
     horns, mocking this bold devil
    with hoarse laughs and black sticks.

    VI   6   IIIIII

A groan from across
      the street.
  Intermittent shrieks
      and screams.
"Don't mind me, If I
    scream at the boys."
      Vagina blurted.
    "Hugo needs to be kept
      in line."
        Can one keep the dead in line?
A triumphant procession of our path
  in the past,
  all bends and mudholes represent.
A crooked, wicked past
  all iniquity, condemning
    our hope, our hopes,
    building with rocky,
      half-dry cement
    our faith, unbending faith.
We smile as we think of the author;
    not the half-wit,
    the doctor; not the sadist,
      the wealthy; not the squalid,
    the calm; not the angry.
History destroys itself,
  as a garden can weed
    itself.
    Rip out its effluvium.


      sieben   7   VII

Harder comic severity
    Strikes my mind.

A whistling wind
   strikes me hard
     as I stride.
Love, Love, Upset,
  follow me, my actions.
My weapons as I walk:
    My Smile; my armour,
    My Howdy; my pike,
    My Laugh; my many fluttering arrows,
    My Jokes; My lovely vaulting steed,
    My Mind; My bag o' tricks.
I have forged these weapons
  in the heat of white coals,
  drawn from a burlap bag,
  fanned by dwarf chimpanzees
They came from the heat gleaming
     to send the water steaming
       as I dipped these beauties
       to capture the colour of heat
      on my weapons, forever
  to have it shine.
Through the shine
  rise bulges,  scrapes
    and bangs.
     Scratches and dents
       from numerous battles
  have rent my armour.
The shapes I made,
    inlaid,
     warped by grime
    and slice
  to show it was not without use.

    And that wind
      the wind whistles

through my mail, my cynicism.


      8    octo    ocho    VIII

Oh most flagrant fragrance on my mind
bending,
sending in to the holy most less.

What seems enchanting-engaging, most enraging
    expunging, punging noteless, bungling -
hoping
    crumbling - most ghost of unheavenly hostess
    ugly toasted wheat crunchies lunching
        on hunches of weedy meads and watery
      reeds struggling against the
            hugger-mugger.


      IX  9  Nine    Novem

I'm a bumbler, a humbler, a crumbler,
tumbler, mumbler, fumbler, and a number.
        Nine is the number of this partition,
          section, division, unit, squadron,
Platoon, part, piece, particle, atom.
    And to my 8 other counterparts,
      What do I owe them?
      Do they hold sway my existence?
      I wish to shrug them off!
        They are now no use to me.
          I am the last and must like string
          hold them together for memory.
        Let them stand on their own!
        Let them distribute ideas fairly!

I have my own part to say.
I'm a bumbler, a humbler, a crumbler,
tumbler, mumbler, fumbler, and a
number.

# To Men, To Make Much of Older Women

Leave my flowers alone, Herrick.
It is my preference
To enjoy a rose in full bloom.

For while a rosebud is small and perfect.
It does not yet yield fragrance.
Or show itself in full.

For though a bloom may miss
A lovely petal or two.
And the bites of bugs may show through.
A little bit of sun burn curl an edge or two.
My preference is the bloom.

Does the rose bud yield to bees or butterflies?
No, its display has only begun.
It needs some time to grow and unfurl
To show the world its true potential.

For two identical buds
May produce two different flowers,
One gorgeous in its plenitude

Another stunted and demure.

So, leave my flowers be, Herrick.
I like my roses to be roses.
I look forward to enjoy them in their ripe and natural poses.

# Gated Community

I've been to your parties.
　Had to announce myself at the gate,
　Driven up to your mountainside driveway.
　Stepped inside your home.

You were sweet, with a beautiful daughter.
　Your husband was gone.
　On business, I guess.
　Your generosity was appealing
　　but I couldn't help ...
　　feeling that if I had the choice
　I wouldn't live in a gated community,
　　walled off from the rest of the world.

I couldn't live in a gated community.
　I have to be part of this world.
　　And, why would I look down my nose at your
　　　　　　　　　　　　　　　lifestyle.
　It just seems so very plain
　That life as it is in your gated community
　Seems entirely too bloody bland.

# 101

You can't push it.
It is immovable.
You can't pull it.
It is ungraspable.

It is too large
to be moved.
It is too smooth
to be held.

But, if you accommodate it,
It is as small as a speck
And can be held on your pinky.

# Autobiographical Poem

I'm from Broadview under the Big Sky.
I never wear a watch but I'm always on time.

# Breath Angel

Breath
Angel
Your air
wakes my sexy crap
dazzles my kisses
in the
deep belly
morning
perfume

Stiff fool,
some cold
blush
fever
throb
makes a
delicious
embrace.

# Race Between Glow and Shadow

It's a race between glow and shadow
In the twilight rosy dusk
Growing, Flying Bat Black
Changes all our sight
Gives us horrid visions,
Challenges, and frights.
Ebbing, crawling Pink Blue
Falls away from Earth
Takes with it our hopes and loves
Stifles cheerful mirth.
And, of course, the glow is losing.
As it does every day
But it will be back tomorrow
To try to fight to stay.

# Richard Brautigan

The Poet lies a Corpse.
He shot himself.
 Lying alone.

His friends stop by,
 Thinking of him.

# Ode to the Moon

The moon streams through my window
  It shines on me and all
   In my dreams it wakes me
    And reminds me of my path
So I start again,
      follow it to my grave
  Knowing it will shine down, once I'm gone.

   Watery teardrops the moon leaves
    From above and below
     Making a mansion
       of Love in kindness
     Slivers of bright
        transcend the night.
If it weren't always there
   We'd have no taste of its beauty
   Tea leaves form an outline
    of a wolf and cub.
      Generous and ruthless.

# Music Box Catalog

Fill the gap
In your life
With crap.

# The Religion of Life

To Give of Myself
And receive from
     another,
In a divine act
   of holy
     communion.

# On the Structural Mechanics of Amor

What is love but
a flimsy whimsy?

# Breakfast

### Bowler
Granola

# The Secret of Life

If you lost your father,
    to be a father.
If you were teased,
    to treat someone with kindness.
If you were beaten,
    to bind someone's wounds.
If you were hated,
    to love someone.
If you were ridiculed,
    to praise someone.
If you were despised,
    to teach someone pride.
If you were called names,
    to show someone their possibilities.
If you were neglected,
    to give someone your attention.

# I was at a

Ramada looking like the food service. All around me there were old women. I sat at a long table getting angrier and angrier. I was looking at my plate and was mesmerized by my meal of gravy, roast beef, and mashed spuds. I don't know why but for some reason I felt my anger becoming intolerable. I had to yell. I did. I let forth with one of my best blahs. BLAAAAAAAAAAAAAAAAAAAAAAAAAAAAAAAAAAAAAAAAAAAAAAAAAAAAAAAAAAAAAAAAAAAAAAAAAAAH! I looked to my left and saw a beautiful girl smile at me. time to destroy. I ran around the Ramada smashing plates and turning table. What? Rico. Rico Paganini stood up. Clean-shaven, well-groomed, and well-dressed with his friend Chainsaw. We began to sing a song about beautiful anarchy and thrash the Ramada. Fun.

# Dawn

Through the night  
Sunshine explodes  
Blasting my skull,  
Pushing the chunks of my head to the ground.

# Maybe

Maybe our love will come to naught.
Maybe naught.

# Clarity+Distinction=Truth

Why do I look at you?
Pale-skinned wonder in blush and shadow,
Lips wrapped 'round
Masticated gum.
You're cute.
You look like a cow.
I love you from a distance.

Your painted nails,
O, to have them rub my flesh.
I wonder.
You'd probably be
"not my type"
So I don't speak,
I only hope,
With no results..

O, your hips
I've seen them walking.
They're connected to nice legs.
Pale, I'm sure.
Rouge, too?

I can only hope
That I will know.

This poem's not done yet.
For your lips,
Your lips are the best.

# Pebble Creek

Make up a ride
On the highway to Silvergate.
Stand around with your thumb
Flying through air.
Stoop down and watch
The wonder bug
Struggle in sun,
Butterfly faces ripping
Pincers from ant's
Bald metal heads.

# Could Desire

Could I paint your eyes
With a cat hair brush?
Make you a dandelion necklace?
Weave you a basket of brown spider silk?
Touch your face with an iris?
Kiss your lips with my lips so hot?
Make you sink into my eyelids?
Warm my hands on your hot stone heart?
Make you smile with desire?

# Journey

The road recedes into itself.
It is too cold this morning,
to tip a car
onto its side.
It just lets itself lay there
With a flowing snowy veil,
Black rubber compressing its spine.

# Love

Wouldn't it depress ya,
To be a waiter with anorexia?

# Andre

Andre and I sat and smoked a cigarette
And drank a beer.
"Shall we fricassee some girls today?
Burn their flesh?
Make them,
Unrecognizable?"
Andre smiled --
That smile.
"I'll get the matches, " he said.

# Electric Lipstick

She was smoking a cigarette,
Electric lipstick
And I saw her in the dull-blinking
Red flash
Of a barroom night-mare.
When she drank her beer
And pulled the loose tobacco smoke
Around her face,
She sent me rolling
Like a pickle on the road
Sour green jelly squirting
Uncontrollably
Onto the painted black gravel.
She kissed the air around her
When she talked.
It drove me mad.
My beer was slipping,
Slipping
Down my throat,
esophagus, stomach burning,
Head melting from the gaze
She fixed on me.

She didn't have to say, "Hello"
Across the room,
I could hear the "welcome"
of nails dancing on wood and glass.
Come here.
Sink into my eyes,
My thighs.
Oh God, she had my soul dancing
On a whiskey bottle
In New York state.
Nowhere among the people,
The loud, low din
Of the people,
Could they see
The meaning of the eyes,
two, tiny images of me
Reflected back.
Would she have me twice over?
She would.
She wouldn't hesitate.
She'd send me careening
Under a Pontiac.
Careening
to my death.
Careening
Into the glowing red butt of her lipstick.

# Song of the Googolplex

Waiting, watching -- outside of my mind,
My memories lurk hoping to find
A break in my thoughts, or to hear
The cogs of my mind intermesh with their
                                            gears,
And it is at these times that they pounce.

A million times a million
Enters my mind.
But no! It erases that and tries to find
A googol times a googol
and that's not enough
As a procession of zeros all strut their stuff.
My mind begins to imagine again
A number that's bigger than none yet been said.
It imagines this number for my, quite some time
And then adds a naught and a naught into line.
The zeros march past for an hour or two
And begin to look like faces of you, you, and
                                              you.

# Ice

The ice on my fingers.
The ache in my brain,
Saliva in my mouth feeling like rain.

Darkness confronts my mind,
In front of my eyes there is nothing but an
                                    empty stage,
Full of chimps loosed from their cage.

No smell, no sound, no feel,
I've died and wondered.

# Drupes and Bribets

The flocculence of the classroom gave way to a
                            rock and four leaves.

Preposterous!
Outrageous!
Can we get to know this ponderous pebble?
In the biblical sense, of course.

A great consternation and several harrumphs
                later the vicar spoke out,
        "A Rock of the Ages."
Everyone knew that he spoke of the death of the
newly fallen leaves and the circular impertinence
of Romance to the modern age.

Bribets?
No, more like a drupe.

# The Gnarled Old Man

The gnarled old man stands in the woods
with           his arms outstretched.
He's not receiving today, they tell you
And you turn and leave past the ancient oak
                              desk.

The gnarled old man stands in his room with
              his arms outstretched.
He's coming down today, they tell you
And the squirrels stop and listen to his sermon.

The gnarled old man stands on his patio with
              his arms outstretched.
Pour me another drink, he tells you
And he sits and cries about the ancient past.

The gnarled old man once stood there with his
                  arms outstretched.
He was chopped down, we tell you
But he lies and cries for the ignorant young.

# Hemlock

What if hemlock were as sweet,
As milk babes suck from mother's teat?

And lilacs' perfume were the scent,
Of rotten carcass in a gamesman's tent.

And if the sight of you were sour,
I would kill myself upon that hour.

# June Rain

The clouds reach long bruised fingers from
                                      sky
And the boy in the hay stares up on high,
Waiting in his mind for the blind hands' touch,
Flowers uprooted to reach for slaking wet,
Inspiring offspring touched by flying buzz
To shake themselves off delirious in the torrent,
Flowing to rest in ground prepared
By the grey waters and lingering white
Of the Fall and Winter's soft delight –
In the sun's enduring blast.

# The Muse Pirates

From the white-washed houses,
Verdant hills, brown green trees
Of the Isle Mnemos,
The Muse Pirates,
Metaphor in scabbard,
See their bandanas
And dread-locked beards
Onto the ship called Empathy.
A song goes up among the crew,
"Pirates Plunder, Murder
And Steal.
Images are the common-lot.
No man has pledge to hoard."
Swirling blue and white to
Purple depths,
The pirates steal this
Image now.
A plundered image
Is set free
And image plunderer
Is freer still
Than verse loosed.

What words are used
To bind us,
Keep us.
These pirates slash
These Gods into
Letters
Lacking meaning.
On darkest shore
False lanterns
Lead the unwary
Verse syndics
To their doom.
In black of knowledge,
These wits
Seek light to
Guide their path,
Receive rocks to
Smash their hulls
From false light
Set inland
By rogues of life,
Thieves of misguided souls.
Hoary hair and eyes shining,
Ripping similes and neologisms,
Breaking the mast of rational thought
And raping the giggling critics.
Shrieks and fire
Rip from below
To fry smiling rosehips
On the literate professors'
Jabbering lips
And nothing lies safe
From the Muse Pirates'
Grasp.
The intellect of the day

Crackles unperturbed
By speech
As it sinks
At the hands of the fearful Muse Pirates.

# Queue

The Man grabs my lock
As I walk on the earth.
He begins to braid
The blinding white hair.
Agh! It pulls at my teeth.
It makes me remember
How I've lived.
Pull me to heaven, O Great One,
Do not forsake me on this planet.
He ignores me with an open mouth and piercing
                                                                       eyes.

He burns the tip of my hair
with his fiery tongue.
It is gold
And shines like the sun in the eye of my foe.
I am life.
I am earth.
I am He.

# The Viking

The viking fights his way to the top
Past the rulers of the mountains
And the diseases of the valleys.
Past the peasants of the fields
And the nobles of the cities.
Past the storms of the land
And the winds of the sea
And cries from an empty throne,
"Where is my victory!
I have earned it," he shouts so that Asgard
might                                              hear.
"For I have conquered the victors of man,
The foes of man,
And the greatest plague on man.

"Where is my victory!
By your oath, I am owed," he screams so that
                              Odin might listen.
"For I have vanquished the rulers of men,
The struggles of men,
And the greatest plague on man."
And as the viking stands,

Silence rains down upon him
And digs deep furrows in his forehead
And creases his cheeks
And the understanding does not come.
Because he, the viking, has been defeated
And he has not yet fought a battle.

# Balanitis

When your acorn
   Gets attacked by a squirrel.

# Blizzard of '03 - Durham

Ice storms trump kudzu.
They certainly are faster.
To kill so many trees in a night.
Of destruction, one is master.

# Prayers Answered

The Heavens opened
And the Rains came.

# They

They are the same as
all of us.
They are different from
all of us.
Exposure to them will
change you forever.
Exposure to them will
leave you the same.
They will change your
manner of thinking.
Your personality is innate
and inviolable.
"The river is constantly changing
and always the same." --

# Missoula Song

Here I am.
My right hand's cold.
Nobody told me it would be
     snowin' today.
But here I am smokin' a cigarette
And watching time pass away.

No place to run to.
No place to hide.
Sometimes I wonder
If God hadn't died.

No place to run to.
No place to hide.
Sometimes I wonder
If God hadn't died.

Here I stand
Watchin' the children
Play the games they
     just don't understand.
But here I am smokin' a cigarette

And watching time pass away.

Walkin' on eggshells
and cryin' inside.
Sometimes I wonder
If God hadn't died.

Walkin' on eggshells
and cryin' inside.
Sometimes I wonder
If God hadn't died.

# To the girl of a different religion who wouldn't date me

Do you think a just
God would deny
   you love?

# 3 Variations on the 1st Line of the Tao Te Ching

The tale that can be told
    is not the tale.
The way that can be weighed
    is not the way.*
The road that can be rode
    is not the road.

---

* Middle stanza is a paraphrase from the translation of the Tao Te Ching by Stephen Mitchell. Translation copyright 1988 by Stephen Mitchell published by Perennial, an imprint of HarperCollins Publishers.

# One More Variation on the 1st Line of the Tao Te Ching

The maid who can be made
 is not the maid.

# Tragedy

The/a slow death of/by cigarette

# Figoa's Law of Irrationality

That religion can be moulded from the flimsiest of circumstances.

# TRAGIC CITY ESSAYS-Number 1
## Muse Pirates in the Tragic City

Tragedy follows this half-hearted city in its minxish attitude toward provincialism, both pastoral and primitive. Constantly being the seductress for the myths engendered by the plains and the lofty pinnacles of the glacier fields, while running away into a metropolitan false dream built on skeletons that are too recently buried; this city plays out its coquetry in linen and plastic and cinder block throughout its final days.

# Sheila

She led me by my standing pole
To where some water filled a hole
And by the great red lake we sat
Dipped a snoos, and had a spat
And wondered where the time had gone,
The time to sit and spit and spawn,
The time to cast and gently feel
A telescoping rod and reel.
The hook took hold its long red gash,
The long and wet began to lash.
The pole's great curve pulled on the wet,
The line's great weight that I should get
To me. I reeled and reeled and spun
Hoping the fish to be properly done.
But fate grabbed the line that May day
And yanked and pulled in its dangerous way.
The pole out of my hand did creep
And I was fearful of the deep.
Sheila grabbed my butt and sunk her feet
To make sure we kept our fishy treat.
But muddy bank caused her to slide,
And her and me we did collide.

Our feet got bunched and, so, we tripped
And into that great red lake we slipped.
About the fish, we did not care,
As we sat and steamed in cool spring air.

# Hello

"Hello," the word slips off my tongue
And I turn around to see no one
Behind me, as usual.
"Hello," I say again hoping somewhere I shall
Hear a refrain.
"Hello. Can anyone hear?"
"Hello. Why does no one answer?"
"Hello. Is anyone there?"
"Hello," the word echoes off the corridors.
"Goodbye."
As I turn and walk away.

# The Dancer

Hey, you're, you're a dancer.
I can tell
By the way
You move.
You want to move closer?
Understandable,
I'm
Touchable.
So you want to touch me?
I don't care,
Just don't give me
Too much
Of what I don't care for.
You want to lie on me.,
Lie to me.
Move your hips some other way; please.
And, of course,
The hands
Connected firmly
To the body
Have a mind
Not of their own.

Do you have a mind?
The wild instincts
Of what-kind-of-metaphor?
Help me out, could you?
Oh, you can help me.
I can help
Myself,
Can I?
I DON'T WANT YOUR FREE LOVE
IT COSTS ME TOO MUCH
And
You've been handing out coupons
On the four-lane black top.
Do you want to be run over?
No you don't have to run over
To me. Have you learned?
I haven't gotten the significance
Of that last act. Maybe, a
Program, players' guide. Who's
Directing this scene, anyways?
Lights
Lights
Oh, don't touch me again.
You move nice.
Hey, I really like the way you move.
Why don't you dance the Jelly?
That was one of my favourites.
I especially liked the part
Where you spread yourself
On the whole loaf of bread.
Food for the public.
We should really get some quality control.
What you've been giving is sweet,
But some people have been
Complaining of a bitter aftertaste.

Disagreeable,
Unsettling.
It, uh, it's cheap.
You know what I'm saying?

# My love

I kiss my love's lips so red, so sweet
And watch her eyes vacuum
my love-filled soul

# Illings

Illings blows shit out its asshole
It's a heartless fuck of a whore
of a town thats dyin to be a city,
So bad, its rude and dirty and heartless
for no good reason and Naggin'
Blue-haired ladies sippin' piss
see out of their rose-coloured eyeballs
all the drunken bums that stumble
dead on the walk beaten by cops
Frozen by Illings Fat Hogs oinking
Down the street followed by Punks
who couldn't remember their age
Yelling at anybody who can't kick
their ass because they're goin 70
to Fuck Fluff Pube Chicks on the Rims
Expending Jism in the only real Jack-off
In this Massive Wanker Villa
Of Tin can Trailer Parks, King Size Stys
And Bland Blandness painted a colour
you hope your neighbor won't laugh at
out of the ground that's fertile
and very arable and concreted over

with baby bottles and monuments
anybody who could be the biggest
asshole and loved and hated
by Yo Mama who sells herself for
a weeks rent and a gallon of wine
in a downtown rosary of Bars that
beep into the night sucking the corpus
slitting their throats to let the air in
or banging the heads on the side
of the boat by a land cursed by all
who live in constipation of the love
that never existed in all the world
but especially not here, not now
in this Broken beer bottle shred
of the silly flat tire you can't
help but get to sign the car
out of order, made to order
for the sheriff's hate and you hate
and its all nothing once your head
comes rolling off after the train
severs it from your body. But your
Body doesn't miss it in this town
to spasm is to be in a provocative lurch
and loose your fluids to fly in so
many faces, Mother and Daughter
that Dad left smiling as he pulled
the trigger and maybe he got out
of this town to see his whirling
eyeballs go spin the puke bowl
From the empty night retching to clear
the air of the stench that sinks
into the gutters of what people here
think is a conscience but is really only
an excuse to not blame themselves
for their own horrid vileness and

the crass crabs happy enough to have
their claws into a meaty morsel that
might have fallen to nurture something
anything that was love that sought
a life of its own in a light of
its own and made something of
clay and made to be alive and
made to be just as dirty as that clay
cause all it ever was was clay
and any airs it ever had was
the bubbles in that clay and someday
that clay'll be pounded flat and all
it'll be is just another layer
in that pancake fiber of soil
skirting that filthy coprolite.

# Poemoep

In order to save this poem,
We must destroy this poem.
Hear us Sing!
In order to love this poem,
we must hate this poem.
Hear us sing!
This poem cannot save itself,
It lacks reason and imagination.
We have these and must help this poem,
Help this poem to its conclusion
As a witty and light piece of verse.
This poem has its flaws and
For this reason it will crack
And break in our brains.
In order to save ourselves,
We must destroy this poem.
A slight reworking, reordering
Is in order.
Order, our sacred vow.
Sense, our sacred weapon.
This poem is an indictment
Of poetry and this must not be allowed.

Or, maybe this poem is an
Indictment of poets, same thing.
Or, maybe this poem is an
Indictment of critics, same thing.
Clarity, our sacred grail.
Clarity, our clarion call.
What the fuck is this poem saying
Any which?
This poem needs neologisms
And creative useage,
A bird might be nice,
Or some plumbing.
This poem is confusing
And confuses us.
Confusion ain't good.
The muse has laughed in this poem's face.
She excreated this thing after a three day drunk.
This thing doesn't deserve to be called a poem.
It could be prose if you out took the breaks.
An orphan thing it was abandoned
Mid-sentence.
Crazy usage pervades this flatulence.
The writer is a moron.
Let us dig him from his primrose grave
To give account for his badness.
The badness that oozes, oozes, and oozes,
And its crippling repetition,
Its hard-hung alliteration,
Its perfunctory personification,
The fawning rhymes,
The languishing lines,
The breaks that come
At terrible places.
The author/voyeur has no taste
And no taste for us.

Flame is too holy for this
And the trash, too ah

# The Branch Crack'd

It's not easy to say
On a cold winter day
What causes a branch to break.
If it wasn't the snow
That it held until now
And it wasn't the hard Northern blast;
Hurling whistling tunes
Through rock-tough dunes,
Causing the rubbery shake.
Wind had blown by before
Back and forth twice or more
Smashing branch to the ground on the last.

Was it slight imperfection
That upon close inspection
Would have proven to pass by your eye,
Or the slow-moving sap
Filling crack and small gap
Striking blown boughs from inside.
It was due, so they say,
To have happened that day
Next on the schedule to die.

But that answer's easy
Derivation quite sleazy
A warm place for fool's love to hide.

No, the answer I seek
Is one hard to speak
And not so much simpler to write.
It deals with the strain
Caused by everyday pain
Crumbling steel shafts into rust.
It's in butterfly wings
Filled with ants' stings
Keeping beauty from flight,
And it dwells in some red
Flowing forth from the dead
Laughing Hollow soul's outer crust.

You can say it's cream,
My answers a dream,
And has avoided the question's jist.
That it's just as lazy
And it'll crush like a daisy,
Under the iron man's boot.
But that attitude's brutal,
A concept most futile,
Causing itself upon itself to twist.
But the branch, it done cracked,
At the least, it's a fact,
And warm words don't amount to a hoot.

# Winter Snuggle

I walk in forest hills, enclos'd by love.
Her breath and fog engulf my hood, my mask,
And keep me gently rob'd by frost and gilt,
Removed from life's grim blocks. My smiling joy
Shines brightly forth to greet my love and have
Her speak, to tell me what her life in worlds
Unknown to God, unseen by many and heard
By me, was like in those last years. We lay
And whine in time, unclock'd, for love's soft quilt
To hide our talk from God's great ear and guilt.

# The Eternal

We languished in spotted groves,
Bidding time to stop and stay,
Remove its scars, ugly moles,
Refresh out patience in days
By sparkling matter, ground grey,
Sprinkled down on faces and eyes,
In love's sentiment combined,
Making a rope, mossy gold.
As our dual-self smiles enthralled
By mesmerism from the stone,
We are, in our plural world
Of groves and groves entwining,
Young in our bond of blank love,
Hanged from death by our rope.

# Torture

Caught by the hands
        Dangled in air
            Scrambling over the match
                                heads.

That stud the ground
        Below my feet,
            Flint on the soles of my shoes.

My head's in a vise
        Great screws in my ear,
            A rusty wrench hangs from my
                                neck.

The handcuffs that bind me
        Rip into the skin,
            Tiny creeks of blood cross my
                                face.

I cry for relief
        Pounded by whips,
            Soaked in gasoline that drips

Down to the match heads
           And I keep my feet raised,
             But my legs are getting weaker.

# Agnosticism

In time I came to know what I knew not;
the complex forms and rioting blocks
Of concise society and murderers shot;
The heartworn cares of cultural shocks
Spread by assassins' hard needles,
Filled with dreamy narcotic sleep,
manufactured on corporate dreedles,
plunging us into the dip with the sheep;
The hard raisins of knowledge
Kept from my outstretched hands,
Lowered beneath the level of mental dredge;
The intricate mystery of my glands,
powering me on to my own fantastic life,
Making me live a question; cut from myself by a
                                                      knife.

# Wind

| WHEN | ALL | WHEN |
|---|---|---|
| LOVE | SONGS | LOVE |
| IS IN | THAT | IS IN |
| THE | I | THE |
| WIND | SING | WIND |

# Shhh! Poet at Work

What am I doing?
    A poem just came into my head.
I wanted to get it down here
    Before I lost the thread.

# Men

Like big, overstuffed babies,
They toddled around from
 one dangled keychain to another.

# Life

Sometimes, I love.
Sometimes, I Die.
Sometimes, I wake
To do it all over again.

# Fragments and Aphorisms

Life is succeeding and failing
with the same decision at the
same time.

They searched around the world
And, when they got home they found
They already had their own sound.

Moonlight settles in the dust
So we can start to play

I thought I was looking at a black
wall. I had been looking at a
white wall but my eyes were
closed.

Those who repeat the mistakes of the past
are condemned.

Parents are God's punishment
for being born.

I have found it much easier to go
through life with an open mind
and a closed mouth.

No matter how cold it gets
Your ass still sweats.

A true perfectionist can stretch
any task to infinity.

When one is slave and one is master.
two souls are oppressed.

The raindrop's mirrored world
splintered
by collision with its image

# Sheila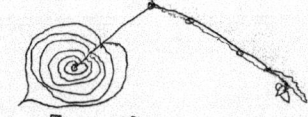

She led me by my standing pole
To where some water filled a hole
And by this great red lake we sat
Dipped a snoos, and had a spat
And wondered where the time had gone,
The time to sit and spit and spawn,
The time to cast and gently feed
A telescoping rod and reel.
The hook took hold its long red gash,
The long and wet began to lash.
The pole's great curve pulled on the wet,
The line's great weight that I should get
To me. I reeled and reeled and spun
Hoping the fish to be properly done.
But fate grabbed the line that Mayday
And yanked and pulled in its dangerous way.
The pole out of my hand did creep
And I was fearful of the deep.
Sheila grabbed my butt and sunk her feet
To make sure we kept our fishy treat.
But muddy bank caused her to slide,
And her and me we did collide.
Our feet got bunched and so we tripped
And into that great red lake we slipped.
About the fish, we did not care,
As we sat and steamed in cool spring air.

## Other Works by the Author

*Party Like a Lacrosse Star*

*Your Healthcare Sucks*

*The Outrider: Collected Columns 2000-2006*

www.ingramcontent.com/pod-product-compliance
Lightning Source LLC
Chambersburg PA
CBHW032007080426
42735CB00007B/533